I0424355

A Poetic Rendition of A Codependent Experience

by
Howard E. Sims, Jr.

Copyright © 2001 by Howard E. Sims, Jr.
All rights reserved.
No part of this book may be reproduced, stored in a retrieval system, or
transmitted by any means, electronic, mechanical, photocopying, recording, or
otherwise, without written permission from the author.

ISBN: 0-75963-440-8

This book is printed on acid free paper.

1stBooks – rev. 05/30/01

However, if the two parties included are inclined toward a relationship based on commitment to one another, complimenting true love, this may only serve to enhance the union.

The cementing imperative for success lies in the dual prerequisites of love and commitment, to each other and to the Saviour and His bonding principles.

The foundation of love-and love itself-is embodied in the Saviour. As with all His promises a successful martial excursion is guaranteed with adherence to His principles of martial cohesion.

Problems arise, at any point, toward division, hostility, and animosity when these principles are overlooked, subordinated, or abandoned. Jesus' doctrines are precepts, infallible. Whether practiced in marriage or other applicative aspects of life, Jesus' principles are sure. Even dealing with the pain derived by one-sided, unfair treatment one may experience his relief. The injured party, by his Grace will endure many times, successfully to the end. With Christ's help, growth, maturity and victory, as he deems, will always be attained.

Ode 32

With unreality I must make a break,

Back to a Godly reality,

Although delivered from addiction's quake,

I retain my emotional maladies.

Trying hard to compensate,

For my "thorn-like" infirmities,

Diligent effort I've tried to make,

for my loss of love continuity.

Though I hate to admit it,

I've fallen short of the mark,

By a margin so far and great,

Although I hate to truly submit it.

Nearly all definitions of love I did break!

But I'll try to relate,

To my fiancé',

A love of commitment and might,

As I do t my Lord and Saviour,

The eternal, Jesus Christ!

Ode #33

The doubt concerning my beloved's love for me,

Leaves my total life,

In ambiguity.

I know she's aware,

But doesn't care to express,

So that I can bare,

This disquieting mess.

Only an occasional thought,

Or a word sometimes kind,

mainly when things are brought,

does she quiet my mind,

Only once maybe twice,

has she expressed in any way,

As though it were a vice

to say, "This is your day."

Only when stressed out,

And nerves clearly burned

Does she reach out,

And express concern.

Why do I have to get sick,
Before she can see,
That I'm human too,
And in need of empathy?

But deep down inside,
I know she's not,
A vocal person,
Unless, put on the spot.
Her overall essence,

Is more than sweet,
With her innate spirit,
Enough to lure and keep me hot.
In spiritual captivation,
And often irate,
With breaks in communication,
With subjects changed,
Often too abrupt,
With apathy,
That makes me want to give up.

But in spite of all this,
I'd be telling a lie,
That with her I'd choose to split.
Knowing I'd rather die.

For knowing what was meant,

Expressed by a professional counselor,

"That i could be miserable with,

Or, miserable without her."

Ode 34

Regardless of what you do,

Regardless of what i hate,

Regardless of whether or not you intended,

To purposely make me irate,

Regardless whether by your own right

Or, with others' in a ploy

You can continue to frustrate me, and attempt to annoy.

But one thing's for certain,

And I'll tell you it's impossible,

If you think it's hard,

My "deliverance" will remain intact,

Because it was the promise of God.

So whether they be purposeful

Or unintentionally related attempts,

In getting your life together,

I no loner resent

Your attempts to make me feel guilty,

Concerning me forecasting your relapse,

For predicted non-maliciously

It's just a response to your ill-trodden path!

Due to my sensitivity,

I used to recoil with hurt,

Time and again trying to help you,

When to your advantage you'd plot more dirt,

In your ultimate life's goals,

Which you don't honestly reveal,

The intentions for yourself and this concinnity,

You choose still to conceal

So if you choose, to continue,

In no one to fully confide,

And your "Biz", you keep on, in your life,

with dark issues to hide,

The hurts, pains, and injustices,

That leave your life hollow,

And you don't have to believe me,

But the void in your life will follow,

you'll, forever, and be where you're at,

Perpetuating for you, your cycle of relapse.

In your "Biz", you haven't learned,

The secret to erase,

The problems in your life,

In the sequence you must face,

It's a biblical imperative,

That at some point you must "stand"

Putting full trust in God,

Understanding too, being accountable to man.

In the form of some individual,

institution, or vehicle,

Given by God, on which you choose rely,

You must put confidence in something or someone,

to the point of being willing to die,

Because a t some point you must realize

For you like all others trying to

Find yourself in God,

Into proper perspective, Let me put it to you!

We all shall leave this world

A fact we view euphemistically,

Thinking as boys and girls

"it's not yet time for me!"

But as decades roll by,

And life's delayed accomplishments make us concerned,

Then sudden realization,

Of years stragically-spurn

For whatever reason

It really doesn't matter,

But through this revelation,

God allows final chances to get it together.

As illnesses complicate our ability to view
And the pictures no longer clear,
To others, and for me and you,
We must hold together, dear.

Some people may suggest, "That
We don't bring God into this",
But because we subordinate him,
Our problems still persist.

Uncovering and dealing prayerfully
With our besetting sin(s)
is the only way to put,
Life's horrors to an end.

Characteristically, I've been there for you
And I really don't regret,
The support and care, i gave was true
And especially the love, you may suspect.

But, this too, you see,
Too Is about me,
You and us-I'm trying to align;
But the introduction of this BuSpar Therapy
has come at a really bad time.

It was bad at first,

Our divisions and hurts,

But now while you

Are in re-hab,

It's cause me to miss court,

I feel a need to abort,

This drug causing me to act so bad.

Through the years you see,

In various drug therapies,,

In myriad methodologies I've sought help;

With my health declining,

And with us aligning,

There was relief like nothing else,

But after six years of trying

my love's not dying

But I'm losing my effectiveness,

My sojourn with you,

Is so very true,

One I will never regret.

I found in you,

A person who,

Is variable as the wind;

But regardless of change and shift,

I'd rather be with you to the bitter end.

After times that fluctuate,

Being joyful and irate,
Times blissful, times of ravage
I'd still choose to be with you,
If you'd still have me too,
This concinnity I hope to salvage.
My paranoia, confusion, and stress,
has nearly gotten the best,
Of my life, those dear, and you,
But there's one enhanced certainty,
I know He won't desert me,
Stumbling and faltering'
Through my venues.

And if at some period of time,
If You read these poetic lines,
For us I tried, caring, sincere and true,
My dear fiancé'
With tears in my eyes,
Know that Howard Sims, Jr...loves you
The Godly things they might not be.

But even though we've parted,
The things that we started,
I pray will lead her to the Lord;
And though I should be finished,
I desire to replenish,
And have our concinnity, in
God restored.

In the past brief separations,

Caused by our frustrations,

Kept my love and me at odds;

But I guess I improperly,

Tried to get to see,

That all I wanted for us were

Things of God!

Apparently I've failed,

In the poor communication that

entailed,

And its certain we'll stay apart;

So in the relationship I messed up,

whatever becomes of us, I leave totally up to

God.

Ode 36

I agonized and despaired,

That my fiancé no longer cared,

And that alas! We were finally through,

My mind subconsciously blurted,

That even God must have deserted,

me, but down inside I knew it wasn't true.

For days no for a week of pain,

Mental stability no longer remained,

With frantic insanity I tried to find'

The one that I loved

Second only to the "Three" above,

As my whole being ached and pined.

Using every day,

In my vast repertoire

I connived, I schemed, and I did plot!

Getting absolutely nothing,

With trickery and bluffing

With professional help still nothing I got.

After staying awake long hours,

In final days I lost all power,

And did what I should have done from the start,

After days, lying down to rest,

For seven minutes at best,

Resigning my fate I saw the power of god.

The phone rang that second,

As though my resigning had beckoned,

And my heart shouted, "I know who that is;"

It was the lady of beauty,

The one love truly,

My fiancé, that incomparable "Kid."

Before resigning, I'd been praying,

Reminding the master, his promises saying,

That if I didn't faint I would reap my goal.

Know the "good work" "He" initiated,

would surely be promulgated,

As Phillipians 1:6 has told!

Howard E. Sims, Jr.

So you see all the worry,
Concerning me and my fiancé
just fruitlessly caused myself
Only to be worked up;
Had I just sat still and waited,
Aligned my will, not lost my faith.
More quietly i would have drunk
From the victor's cup!

Ode 37

It appears to me,

The place for me,

Is Murphy's on Madison Avenue;

Because I'm here,

Not with my dear,

Appears the best I can do.

Disappearance issue now not involved,

At this time its been resolved,

But the tension mounts and goes on'

Because now I don't laugh

When speaking to my other half,

because of her current eerie undertones.

I remind myself she's just beginning

To spiral out, a life unfitting,

And still there's an ever-present schism;

From it we will both have to drag,

Undertaking a brand new path,

Leaving behind, we two, all negative isms.

But as in the past we have relied,

Or else this concinnity would have died,

And the factor of reliance was in God;

so when things get eerie I'll keep depending,

On Christ to prevent us from ending

When matters between us get difficult and hard.

From it we will both have to drag,

Undertaking a brand new path,

Leaving behind, we two, all negative isms.

But as in the past we have relied,

Or else this concinnity would have died,

And the factor of reliance was in God;

So when things get eerie I'll keep depending,

On Christ to prevent us from ending

When matters between us get difficult and hard.

Ode 38

Now I find,

My role redefined,

One that I meditate over and muse

After I scrutinize, I realize,

Even now I can't be amused,

With our nemesis gone,

My job is to prolong,

Its abstinence so it will permanently stick;

One method for us,

May be found in A.A.

But certainly, in the source book

Of Phillippians 1:6.

We must proceed with caution,

Never getting the notion,

never walking upon the camouflaged

latent triggers,

Because farther along that track,

Should we fall and look back,

Our demise shall be seven times bigger.

But this time our support,

To help us abort,

comes in a more willing reliance upon God;

And our success is guaranteed,

As in sixteen years seen,

In my "deliverance" toward him I prod.

A moment at a time,

My beloved will find,

Her confidence and assurance

Will grow;

With retained victory over,

Minor trigger's that used to

Throw her, God-reliance will increase, and

her fears will go.

Erroneously feeling subordinate,

There'll be no avoiding it,

I'll lovingly help everyday;

We'll both get through,

And with God's promises too,

moment by moment in this

Regard I'll pray.

Ode #39

If it was a brush with death,

Quiet-as-it's kept!

It could have been kept from me;

Knowing I'll have to go,

Someday I'm told,

for right now it's bad timing, you see.

For now there's breaking

A great comeback in the making,

for me and my fiancé;

but the things for us I'm planning,

may now be landing,

Days, maybe weeks away.

If hospitalization is required,

At the doctor I've arrived,

It's certain we'll miss our appointments,

But we'll have a break through,

I know it's true,

We'll get God's blessings and his anointings.

He said, "All things work together,"
For those, under His love that gather
Although more than a delay it might seem,
Be it hours, days, or weeks,
his kingdom we will seek,
And ultimately our good we'll redeem!"

Ode #40

If we can fight throughout our lives,

To attain through struggle and constant strife,

That we know and believe,

That which is most significant to achieve;

If one can endure day by day,

In spite of what friends an foes say,

A harmony within self,

Despite trials or anything else.

And most of all when drawing a blank,

At all times to give thanks,

When times are good or times are hard,

To our vehicle, and our goal, God;

To see in our fellow man

All the good that we can,

While relying only on "His" help

to sustain integrity of self;

We'll know in moments hollow,

Regardless of the circumstances that follow,

The fact that we've been true,

To our self, and our God, too.

And that, if not for you, but for me,
Spells integrity,
The uncanny ability,
To sustain a march of reality;
the ability to persevere,
When life's trials are ominous and unclear,
Even when one's dears
Suddenly desert and disappear;

to keep focused on one's goal,
When there's torment of the soul,
Then only in Christ be bold,
In restoring and keeping one's hold.

Because in some things, all may veer,
Not keeping one's focus perpetually clear,
But truly broken, with His guidance near,
Lost of integrity, one need not fear.

In life's issues that really matter,
Most of us, if we could, would really rather
have placed upon a silver plater,
A success that would not tear and tatter.

But our Creator has so designed,

That in this life we can never find,

A consistent integrity so inclined,

Without our wills and

His aligned.

But once in such area of my life very dark,

With Christ's help I now sustain an integral march,

With my primary aim now to impart,

For others, the course, that for me, He once did chart!

The impetus for me is given from above,

His grace descending like a dove,

To unite those in need as the fingers of a glove,

In the harmony of A.A. fellowship and true Christian love,

But regardless if other's success is aided by me.

I know through A.A. and my efforts in Christianity,

He'll keep in my members and throughout me,

The honor and continuity of my

Sobrietal integrity.

Ode # 41

We can buck and kick,

Scratch and sit,

Even be aggressive and claw;

But we won't move forward,

While being froward

Moving contrary to God's law.

If we just sit back,

And refuse to spat,

And one another's point try to see;

and intelligently discuss,

the discrepancies between us,

It will reduce conflict's intensity.

Whatever we do,

The inclusion of God too,

Is not an option in which we might or may;

Because there'll be perpetual schisms,

not employing God's wisdom,

In an empathetic, caring way.

Of Forgotten Origin

We've ended this time,
With a little different "kick,"
But I assume responsibility,
for the finality of our split.

I'm truly not being flipped,
In making the above remark,
But I'll forever maintain the conviction,
That "crack," was our nemesis from the start.

It's difficult for protagonists to see,
Their vast disparities,
That ultimately broke down trust,
Creating confusion, such as between us.

But this time I'm not seeking pardon,
For as a co-dependent I've learned,
For that the last six years of my effort,
Of my love for you was spurned.
For in the way it ended,
It shall forever be on my head,
In attempts to bring some order,
I brought tragedy instead!

Howard E. Sims, Jr.

I could blame it on the heat,
Or the combined ailments in my life,
Or the stress of attempting to maintain,
Six years of a hypocritical life!

Vocalizing one doctrine,
But in reality, living a lie,
with the mark totally missed;
Once hoping with all my heart, I tried;
to elevate from an abyss,
A most unseeming couple,
Too late seeking-total help from God,
found ourselves too deep in trouble!

But I'll never truly blame you,
for under the circumstances;
You did all you could'
To interpret my jumbled message,
Not communicated as it should.

You said you thought my goal,
Was to happily marry you,
Now I must tell you so,
This is only partially true;

And though it may appear a lie,

In light of recent events,

without expulsion of "crack" and adding God,

Our plans would only be wrenched.

I know this is our last round,

In defeat I have found,

In a final act of exasperation,

I made hopeless our collective situation,

making a total mess,

For us, the worst instead of the best!

Whatever you and others think,

You can recollect from the start,.

About you, the Master shall never let sink,

"The thoughts and intents of my heart!"

Howard E. Sims, Jr.

Untitled

Upon release,

Things still incomplete,

But still the way they were;

I hope my suspicion,

That moving into remission,

Are not negatives losing significance

In a blur!

The impact of Christ,

In the dungeon, those nights,

Manifested and made itself known'

Spurting from my mouth,

And in situations about,

my faith not only increased but has grown.

My "deliverance" is sure,

Christ making recovery pure,

And to Him I am extremely grateful;

For as it was there,

I find here,

I'd not trade Christ, for gold by the crate full.

But there's still an uneasiness,

As I flow with life's currents,

And try to make sense out of my experiences;

Finding in my blunders,

And my successes too, I wonder,

Not any more appreciating the differences!

Through the vast disparities

Of life deceits and charities,

There's a "ripple-effect" touching all;

Making lucid and all certain,

That no one has his own burden

And without an inner-link we're

all bound to fall!

So in sporadic moves from confusion,

to success' illusion,

There's only one calming thought that shall suffice;

That my helper,...very personal,

Assisting me,...universal,

Is the one and only, Lord Jesus Christ!!!

Howard E. Sims, Jr.

Untitled

It always appears that the end is near,

When there's conflict at a relationship's seams,

When couples overreact,

To a comment or act,

And for them allow it to come between!

But what are they to do,

That imperfect two,

That God, Himself put together;

To continue to try,

And one another not, to deny,

As their lives, they attempt to better.

But the issue of commitment,

Embodied in the conviction,

Of godly love, above anything else;

should be possessed by each,

during relational valleys and peaks,

to keep the union in touch with itself!

Empathy is essential,

And shouldn't be just coincidental,

Within the inherent fabric or a union's bond.

With such a glue, concinnities start anew,

When threatened by separation's harm.

One another cherish most,

And in God only boast,

For your relationship's inception and longevity;

and always realize,

That any escape from demise,

Is due God, not really you and me!

Howard E. Sims, Jr.

WHERE ARE THEY?

Where are they,

When you have nappy hair,

When you're all flustered,

What do they care?

In the wee hours of night,

When you have hunger,

That's not just an appetite, it's addictions thunder

when the times you consider,

Lying flat on your back,

For the procurement from others,

Your nemesis,... "Crack?"

When the interaction in your anatomy,

Becomes incompatible,

And your whole being cries

For the nearest hospital?

You run, escaping your circumstances,

and find yourself stuck,

When you want to return,

Do they ever show up?

Do they ever enlighten you spiritually,

if so, without an inward frown?

Do they console empathically,

When emotionally, you're going down.

Do they breathe in your being,

A true desire to try,

To accomplish an objective,

for which only a saint would die?

To stick by your side,

In whatever circumstances may render,

Do they not run and hide,

And your forward progress hinder?

And...

Who, to you, does cleave,

Regardless of mistakes,

And promises not to leave,

And you, never to forsake?

Where are they?

Ode 35

This August 21st of 1998,
For me it's become apparent,
At 5:11 AM, be it early or late,
Her love's become inerrant!

For six long years,
I had my fears,
With perpetual and unending ambiguity;
But though I've lost, and paid the cost
She'll always be dear to me!

I hope she finds just what she wants,
That she could not find in me;
But her tendency to deceive,
Leaves me to believe,
She never did,......indeed.

THOUGHT,...

Pain in relationship, in one or both parties, due to a temporary or permanent schism, is viewed by some, as overly emotional, or a degree of sensitivity on a scale sometimes approaching masochism.

Query, Agony, And The Cup

It's not at all to you odd,

That I query you God,

"Cause sages throughout the eons,

Have so done,

And as they, I know you can,

Be mindful of man,

But at times I don't feel you to be,

Eternally mindful of me.

In spite of evidence to the contrary

Your compassion seems to vary,

With life's pleasures waxing and waning;

I find myself to you crying,

Feeling as though I'm dying,

Being vexed and forever complaining.

It just doesn't seem to be,

clinging to your strengthening cup.

For in it I can always retrieve,

The strength to believe,

And the power to just more than cope;

for contained in your chalice,

Is the removal of all malice,

And is the contents of my life's total hope.

While thinking I was most miserable,

By the despair caused by my foibles,

With my life depicting excruciating agony,

I wondered why i couldn't find,

As in your cup so sublime, despairing sea!

An extractor out of life's,

But life could not drown completely,

The taste which so sweetly,

Pouring from cup which was to suffice;

It was then I knew,

In the essence so true,

The delivering power of Jesus Christ.

Ipso facto from Him being unable to depart,

I press steadily toward the mark,

knowing His power is unable to fail,

not sipping, no I gulp,

From this glorious cup,

Now knowing that I'll surely prevail.

Howard E. Sims, Jr.

So when clouds of gloom and self-pity,
Insidiously envelope me.
When blows of life render me giddy,
And knock me to my knees.
When imaginations make things appear
That they're much worst than they are,
And the reality of things that are dear,
Are indeed greatly worst by far,– –

i will not query you Lord of host,
I'll do as I done in times past,
i will draw upon your cup the most.
And until the day of the Lord I'll last!

Untitled

As life presses on,

And our saga is prolonged,

With its intricacies progressing faster;

Up from life's abuse we've been raptured,

By the Holy Spirit, been captured,

and it's all due to Christ, the Master.

For my beloved others, and I,

Many tears I have cried,

In vain attempts our lives to straighten out;

Employing my own strength,

In most of the attempts,

In myself alone I have doubt.

For historically I've seen,

We've only been redeemed,

When we've tenaciously employed the Saviour;

When by providence led,

Rather than our own might instead,

We prayerfully altered our behavior.

It's been proven we can expedite,

Deliverance from our plight,

If Biblical principles we employ;

And continue to sustain,

All efforts in Jesus' name,

To eventually pass through heaven's door.

In the past six years,

It' become perfectly clear,

with the help of a God-given mate;

In my beloved, you see, was given to me,

A spouse to help elevate;

me from a sobrietal comfort zone,

To "deliverance's" throne

Which I find a much more blissful state!

Some ordeals were intense,

In "crack-houses" i spent,

The majority of the past six years;

As my diamond in the rough,

By her side I thought I must

Stand vigil, despite my fears.

In continued venues, I hope

Strength does increase.

As we converge at the Master's feet,

As I gain faith and commitment to go on'

In spite of carnality, and the "enemy,"

And lives additional difficulties,

I see on the horizon, the beauty for which I longed.

For surely if and I had not,

On a portion of Damascus'

block,

Had our destines not entwined and embraced;

In such an ephemeral span of time,

The love we did find.

May surely have never taken place.

So on this plane of corporeality,

In self correction and restoration I'll spend

For other's having empathy

In Jesus' name,....AMEN!!!

Howard E. Sims, Jr.

Deliverance: From a co-dependent's "perspective"

First and foremost for "deliverance,"
We find, initiator, vehicle, and goal,
Is the imperative of abstinence,
For the liberation of one's soul.

Abstinence is the catalyst,
That makes possible everything else,
couples with prayerful maintenance and God,
shall inevitably sustain them self.

Sometimes hour by hour,
and at times day by day,
Abstinence will feed off its own power,
And in Christ never go away.

So approaching your coveted recovery,
Listen to God and the candor of true friends,
Then an uninterrupted sobrietal trek,
You'll possess, that shall never end

For once abstinence is initiated,
You best never look back,
No matter the negative chemical,
Be it beer, "pot", or "crack,"

Ask God, always, to grow spiritually,
To enhance your ability to discern,
The total truths concerning sobriety,
Embracing all lessons you'll learn.

And remember too, on the continual plane,
In this life and the next, I'll be there,
With the Father, Son, and Holy Spirit,
For you, empowering me to care.

Receive Christ's promises, and ever be confident,
That our "deliverance" develops as it should,
'Cause for those that love and repent
All things shall work out for their good.

I used to worry if you knew this fact,
But your spirit was cognizant from the start,
Impacting around me the way you act,
Birthing love in both our hearts.

Though have been times for this concinnity
I've almost become a mourner,
But when things have turned for their worst,
i persisted in your corner.

Howard E. Sims, Jr.

Each Day Is A Gift From God

Each day is a gift from God,

As seem from a glance

A new place to start,

At life a fresh chance,

A chance to recover,

maybe,...from a life of error,

With the help of Christ,

A new chance to recede,

From bad habits, that expedite

The life they impede.

A new chance to address,

That which is positive and real,

To embrace and possess,

his promises and build,

The character that he would have us develop,

And put into check,

The addictions that envelope,

And hold us back.

Each day is a gift from God,

For you and I,

To not make so hard,

To let negatives die.

A new chance to embrace,

The lessons from above,

To look into Christ's face,

And each other to love.

Because new days are growing short,

And not left are many.

Soon they shall abort,

Til there are not any.

Howard E. Sims, Jr.

"After A Moment Of Jealousy"

We all have an outlet,
to relay our point of view,
Of relieving discomfort,
And justifying remedy too.

And having pre-determined,
The discomforts to one's self,
That tolerance in these areas
is not up to anyone else.

When friend nor professional.
Can perceive our source of pain,
To us doesn't make it minimal,
But intensifies the same.

It's only strange we find,
Minimizing the discomforts of another,
But when we're neglected and left behind,
At our peer's apathy we shudder.

It could just be in me
That my own sensitivity.
Has by myself, been hyper-magnified,
for years in the voices,
Of "friends" and other sources,
I tried to find solace only Christ provides!

It may take a length as long,
to reverse the years of many wrongs,
Done by sin and carnal abuse'
Though the battle may rage,
Christ has set for me the stage,
for this soldier to never give the
Enemy a truce!

Though others may never understand,
The unreasonableness of my demands,
And also created when my triggers flare,
Whether or not, my pain, wanes or stops,
For others...emphatically I'll still be there!

For I've found through the years,
In the shedding of tears,
in the degenerate life of a prodigal;
That I intensified my own pain,
Trying to gain, and retain,
The contingencies of a life truly horrible.

But through the Grace of Christ,
I've discovered a new life
Based on Godly sacrificiality;
Gaining peace and contentment,
Through empathy, not resentment,
Now, I try to just let my life be!

For I've learned my lesson
That my happiness and blessings,
And self-worth,
Are birth by my acts of benevolence;
Finding true meaning in the above,
a demonstrative life of love,
Depicting spiritual import and relevance.

Ode #1

This is just an ode,

For you and me

Let it be calm and serene,

So that I may see,

A working of your power, Lord,

Without strife, or tragedy.

An expression of your might,

A day of planning, for victory.

Ode #2

Christ is the vehicle,

to our Christ-like goal,

He is the miracle,

For the salvation of our souls.

He's the only means to break free,

From a world of sin that confines,

And if we truly see,

Our lives, with his, we'll align!

Ode #3

The day is nearly done,

And I nearly forgot,

To praise with my pen, the One,

Who delivers me from my spots.

But if nearly I did neglect,

Due to the day's ambivalence,

I truly do suspect

The Holy Spirit, brought it to

My Remembrance.

Ode #4

My day has started out, with a blase' doubt,

In the anticipatory fulfillment of yesterday's plans,

But unlike others, today, I won't smother myself,

And leave the day in the Master's hands,

For my misery, you see, has been for me,

My own destiny to try and construct,

But through the years I've learned,

Not aligning to His word,

My days I only mess up.

Ode #5

With Thanksgiving I approach you Lord,

But it shouldn't be, when I'm okay or just bored.

In adversity and turmoil, I should always thank you, Christ,

Knowing that for all occasions gratitude to you will suffice.

When pain and anguish are unbearable,

You make any situation reparable.

So in peace or misery,

I thank you Saviour for caring for me.

Howard E. Sims, Jr.

Untitled

In the lack of commitment,
We can most surely tell,
The ephemerality of duration,
In most concinnities shall entail.

When one party's uncommitted,
We know of course,
That this is the impetus,
For most divorce.

The inability to endure,
is usually known for sure,
To impede growth and productive change;
And if we don't commit,
And to one another and submit,
Our bickerings shall remain the same.

It's not really odd,
That, without God,
And a lack of serious commitment to him;
We seek in vain,
Our lives to change,
And our chances are truly slim.

After time passes,

And uncertainty still lasts,

Love's viewed as being insincere

And vicarious;

But if by one party, or both.

There's reason for hope,

Struggling not to give,

In viewing

The union nefarious.

It's not only yourself your vex,

not knowing from one moment to the next,

Being undecided, vacillating, and froward;

At some point soon you must,

Make a commitment about us,

For only this way, with God's help move forward.

I hope you see this time,

That this isn't just another.

And in deciding we can commit

Ourselves to common needs;

But until this step is done,

Concerning our being one

how on earth with our life can we proceed?

For some time ago; the above,

I concluded concerning you; in Godly love,

making a vow, compelled by my

heart to be with you for life;

But if, with me you do not feel,

I'm the entity on which you're to build,

You should search for it (or Him),

In the name of Christ!

Decisions concerning any chore,

Is just like fighting a war,

Being unable to decide to engage or to retreat

But if you're able to decide,

I'll fight, in life, by your side,

And with Christ, I know any enemy we can defeat.

Beloved, I can neither fake it or hide it.

For in love, some time ago I decided,

And know the power of the lack of commitment, to hurt,

But regardless of the indecision in you,

I'll continue to love and be there for you;

Irregardless if it's me, you ultimately dessert!

So when you subconsciously or knowingly pass blame,

and however long your inconsistency remains,

I'll pray for us, and with Christ's help, my love, for us, make due;

For it's one truism that's decided,

I'll make adjustments, and in

my love I won't hide it,

And like the master, I'll never

Leave nor forsake you!

Ode #6

The essence of love is loyalty,

Found in the conviction,

Of complete trust and faith,

Without ambivalence or suspicion.

That level of trust, between us,

We never can achieve; in any place,

As it is when we embrace,

In the Saviour in whom we believe.

Thyllida and I: The Flourishing of a Father/Daughter Relationship

By her I've been blessed,

My only child I did neglect,

But loved her in my heart, down through the years;

And I would change some things, if I could,

And would have loved her the way I should,

Not exempting her to the priority of my peers.

She's a classic diplomat,

In handling all my grandchildren's spats.

Imparting to me, the sagacity of the sages too;

there are also times I can remember,

When her voice was soft and tender,

her essence echoed, "Dad, I need to hear a word from you!"

I have very strong suspicions,

That providence orchestrated conditions,

Of a semi-passable chasm between me and my daughter;

Neither, really trying to spurn.

From each other, we now have learned,

Blood's much thicker than water.

Through the years our relationship has grown,

Slowly, by seeds that have been sown,

Now by the Holy Spirit our concinnity approaches

That which it oughta;

For Thyllida, you see,

Exhibits the Christian empathy,

That makes me more than proud to

Say she's my daughter.

Dedicated to my daughter
With Christ-like /fatherly love

Ode #7A

When it appears it's over,

I'm able to cope,

When I'm given signals of your might;

Regardless of plight I'm given hope,

In your sovereignty, Lord Jesus Christ.

It's only through you, that I may anticipate optimistically,

The beauty in all my circumstances,

At times not to my liking; but oh! So realistically,

I have the assurance, 'The outcome's in your hands."

Ode #7B

In my demise,

You've constantly arrived,

Placing in my hand, sweet victory;

After times running around,

Even in the abyss there's the sound,

Of the hoofbeats of your calvary.

When I'm about to give up hope,

I continue to cope,

Because of your aid in my memory;

In ordeals seemingly prolonged,

I'm able to hold on,

Because Christ, I recall what you've done for me!

"Twilight At The Pipe Table: An Eve'-Morn' At Pat's"

The evening terminated as it commenced,

Like all evenings every since,

And I found my acquaintance with

Phyllis it's start.

But before my trek was initiated,

I did not know my strength would be satiated,

And the finality that my morn-eve would be hard!

It seems my dreams of change,

Have been shattered, and no longer remain,

In the negative influences in which I now abide

But regardless of the mess,

Caused by this ill-fated quest,

My experiences I give to Christ, not to hide!

Now a joust just arose,

Insidiously between Pat and me,...now foes,

With each other engaged in a spiritual wrestling match,

But regardless what happens here,

My Saviour shall be dear,

And the negatives here, I'll leave to rest!

For whatever here I find,

I shall always be inclind,

To continually seek my Saviour's glorious face;

For whatever, here they converse,

In their esoteric verse,

The messages of Christ I'll forever embrace.

So regardless of their united schemes,

The power to redeem,

Shall always be a demonstration of His might;

So as with the archaic flood,

Their demonic voices are just mud.

Always subject to the power of Jesus Christ!

But I would like to make peace,

With these, my bretheren, in the street,

But whatever happens here I shall acquiesce;

But it's a pleasure having met,

My brother, Phyllis and Pat,

But my relationship with Christ shall always be best!

Ode #8

In Christ, we sometimes must,

Persist in love, even when there's a lack of trust,

To help a loved one even when,

They're caught inside a vortex of sin,

When their chance of redemption seems small,

And while helping them we are about to fall,

We can hang in there with all our might,

When our efforts are buttressed by the spirit of Christ!

Howard E. Sims, Jr.

Ode #9

Terribly, I've sinned, Oh! Lord; and have not kept,

Your statues in an attempt to help,

The one I love so desperately,

Only moving her away from "You" and me.

Lord help me come closer to You and stay,

Assist also my fiancé,

Whether together or apart,

To put you first my sovereign Lord!

Ode #10

The inconsistencies of love,

Are not necessarily from above,

In trying hard in our own might,

Our relationships we, at times, spite.

But if we back off a bit,

And of our own power quit,

We'll allow the spirit of God,

to complete our union's job.

Ode #11

My visitations with Dr. Black,

Are just as much of a fact,

Of a Godly intervening miracle;

As a method of God,

Processing sin from the heart,

In an worldly-moded vehicle.

It may seem strange but it's true,

The lover's of god are due,

everything that God has promised He would,

So by whatever method,

Those He's selected,

All things shall work out for their good!

Ode #12

Justice administered by man,

Is delivered as fairly as it can,... "yet,...

Not to be compared to God's,

Who knows the thoughts and intents of our hearts,... "He,"...

Can unbiasly discern

Whether a lesson was learned,... "See,"...

Christ has the uncanny ability,

In the sagacity of His sovereignty,... "That we,"...

Draw upon in our time of need,

Relying upon only His mercy,... "Finds the,"...

Fact of our Father's justice makes us inclined,

Our will with His to align!

Howard E. Sims, Jr.

Ode #13

In the U.S. of A. we should always face,

And recognize the beauty of God's grace,

And know that in leadership we've now been smitten;'

Being cognizant of this very fact,

That in our guide book, red and black,

Our progressive path's been written;

In a culmination of events,

Ethical and moral structures have been bent,

By one we did exalt as a leader;

Some knowing from the beginning,

We all now find Clinton sinning

Knowing from the start he was a breecher.

Ode #14

The practically of pragmatism,
Can eliminate our relational schism,
And provide a vehicle back to reality;
For only in a sincere attempt,
From our negatives will we become exempt,
As we try honestly to discover you and me.

In the past, asking what to do?
Created a chasm between me and you,
Walking two different paths to make our "us" right.
But with me you'll always find,

That my path attempts to align,
With my Lord and Saviour Jesus Christ!

Ode #15

Unlike my Saviour,

I must confess, I was late,

Composing this Ode,

On an inappropriated date,

Unlike His promptness,

I did neglect,

And a lack of discipline;

You may suspect!

But I do thank Him

My Saviour God,

For allowing me,

To tackle the job,

My Lord's punctuality,

Is not in it,

But by His grace,

I now complete and submit!

Ode #16

Unlike the triad God-head

Completely foreign to them.

When we're late or fallen,

We must get back up again.

Because to grow and mature,

Within ourselves we must compete,

And show as long as there's breath,

There's no defeat!

Through out the scriptures,

Some of the miraculous appears not hard,

As with David,

Small challenges were his start,

And if we're quite like Joseph,

We will develop the integrity,

to eventually assume,

Greater responsibility!

Howard E. Sims, Jr.

Untitled

Oh! Father God!

Oh! Jesus Christ!

Your prophetic messages abound;

In these end times, we now do find,

Establishment of your prophecies world round!

People are killing,

And people are stealing,

With even daughters against mothers;

Abominations have come,

Even between father and son,

With respect dwindling, too, between brothers!

Oh! My God!

Oh! Father God!

Is it that these things must;

Necessarily be,

to test Christian loyalty

for you, and between us.

For as morality wanes,

And ethics become bane,

And perversion pollutes the world;

Hymns the remnant sings,

With their study of scriptures shall bring,

A treasure like a Mother Pearl.

In the person of Christ,

Is the elimination of pestilence and vice,

And destruction of all wiles and schemes;

But in the end time there'll be many,

Who'll have no faith, if any,

and only a remnant shall be initially redeemed!

If peoples' sins aren't relieved,

And in Christ have not believed,

They'll be caught up in the tribulations, wake;

And for giving the appearance,

In pseudo-adherence,

They will be judged as end time apostates.

So the only thing to save,
One from a eternal grave,
Is a loyal/dependence on the Son;
Discerning biblical truth,
Nurtured from our youth,
As matured disciples stretch
Toward the Son.

Ode #17

Holy Spirit continue to guide,

And terminate rightness in my own eyes,

Help me to continue to more clearly see,

The path leading to my true destiny,

Your vehicles' are the to goals for me that will expedite,

Let me implement, immediately, with Christian might,

and all relationship current, and that I may come in,

Like Paul, let me be another champion against sin.

Howard E. Sims, Jr.

Untitled

It comes to mind,
From another time,
A sagacious point once exclaimed;
By a friend who would repeat,
Everytime we would meet,
Bernice, was her name.

She would reverberate, "it's me oh! Lord!"
Not my sister, my mama or dad,"
In each meeting she said it so much,
It began to make me mad!

But I guess for me,
I was subconsciously,
Grasping the truth of what Bernice said'
My sins were actually attributed to me,
Not by my sister, my mom, or dad!

It's taken the bruises of life,
And unsuccessful fights,
Attempting to deliver myself and others from sin;
Trying to assist God,
In something he started,
Trying really to out-glorify Him!

Soon I started to blame,

Almost anyone who came,

to my mind, for my process of sin'

Discovering the truth,

Not found in my youth.

I began to examine within!

I did begin

to have increased acumen.

While studying God's word;

But I soon realized,

Old habits wouldn't die,

Just by reading and by what I heard!

My youth was full of advantages,

I never quite managed

In the sagacity of the scriptures;

A more blessed life I've missed.

After years in sin's abyss,

Not relaying to the Master's big picture!

But I won't let Satan.

No manner how blatant.

He insidiously tries to implant;

Messages to diffuse hope,

'Cause with Christ I can cope,

For I realize for eternity, I now take a stand!

Howard E. Sims, Jr.

No it wasn't my sister, nor my mother or father,

Nor even that mischievous neighbor,

nor the enemy with the knife,

Who threatened my life,

Trying to give Satan a victory to savor.

It wasn't the years, in

Alcohol and drug infested dens,

And the escapades in them that ensued;

but was by his grace,

That I did escape,

As I now do in current venues.

"A Prayer for Deliverance"

I have a besetting sin,
That did insidiously begin,
That now borders on an addiction;
But because I'm carnal,
With it I did fondle,
And now it's a sure affliction.

At first because I was bored,
And I avoided the Lord,
A deadly demise I now do see;
In the initial fun,
If its course does run,
A wretched man I'll be.

But like Paul,
On the Lord I call,
To deliver me;
Cause in my own power,
Regardless of the hour,
My own self I can't free

Oh! Lord!

Oh! Lord!

Oh! Heavenly Father!

The Father of all nations;

In Jesus' name,

The victory I claim,

To rid me of this temptation!

I know you can,

Your "delivering" hand,

Allowed me an addiction to quit;

Just as before,

You can do it once more,

Through scriptures like Phillippians one/six!

I implore you Father God,

Silently and out-loud,

To deliver me from this tempting game;

so i can assist others,

To help one another,

and more be delivered in Jesus name!

Ode #18

An uncertain beginning,

To a desirable ending,

Is just about to commence;

The initial results,

In General sessions court,

Shall be determined by Providence.

The lessons I've learned,

And the experience earned.

At times seemed very hard;

But upon my mind's been embossed,

These venues of the cross,

And have increased my love for God!

Thought:

The key to avoidance of this, or similar circumstance is strict as possible adherence to relational standards and ethics.

Reasonable healthy self-concern and indulgence may and will assure self-sacrificial approaching of others in more mature, less martyristic light! The idea is balance. Not to overly subordinate self in a samarianic-martyr-like complex, or approach to life, in attempts to compensate for realized, or submerged guilt complexes.

As in all areas of life, balance is mandatory. Insidious self-neglect may definitely be a detriment to sincere Samarianic efforts.

"The State of Tennessee"

The State of Tennessee,

Vs., you and me,

And probably not just us;

There appears to be some discrepancies,

In this system that would try us.

We're put in line,

could pay a fine,

In a system that's inclined,

To make us do time,

To reasonably assure,

That the indigent and poor,

Shall sorely, if at all endure,

In a system that's anything but pure.

It's a sad, sad thing,

When mankind's justice brings,

A mockery to God's perfected plan;

But being reasonably sure,

We have to endure,

With the variation of God's we have at hand.

Howard E. Sims, Jr.

The State of Tennessee,

Vs. you and me,

Trying us when there is strife;

Is indicative of the confusion and disarray,

Encompassing most aspects of life.

On the bench a symbolic head,

By which we're to be led.

To settle myriad disputes;

Evidence of one kind,

Attempting to undermine,

One another also to refute!

But the facts still remain;

that justice retains,

It's ultimate foundation from

The morality of the Lord;

But whatever you do,

The State of Tenn. vs., you,

We should always try to avoid!

> Adopting Salvador Dali's, on the spot "Napkin Theory", the above was written during an actual State trial.

Ode #19

As the ebb and flow,

Of my life goes,

Things seldom just look pale;

Just for me,

nearly daily,

There's a zest my life entails.

This spree,

Is created by he,

Who set all things into motion.

And I survived,

Because He too derived,

I needed his kind of commotion!

Howard E. Sims, Jr.

Ode#20

Oh! Lord!
Oh! God!
I praise your Holy name;
In conflict strife, and peaceful bliss,
Your empathy has remained the same.

In spite of my wavering,
And Satan's lure,
My carnal playing
And at times being unsure,
Of myself, I can't cope,
For in you only
I have hope.

Ode #21

We found a way,

With God's help today,

Killing Satan's attempts to postpone;

Attempts of the devil to interfere,

with that Which is saintly and dear,

Our past nearly realized, very soon, shall now be known!

It was a very vicious fight,

Which Satan waged with all his might,

Especially when our resolve did decline,

But for my fiancé and I,

On the Master power we do rely,

and His strength has kept his will and ours aligned!

Irregardless of the test,

We know whose kingdom's the best,

Being quite evident through the course of history;

Though Satan's forces taunted and boasted,

Conquest was denied his demonic host,

With my fiancé and I now forecasted the victory!

Howard E. Sims, Jr.

The promises of scripture are truly real,

Even with opposing forces that kill and steal,

If one only persists and doesn't stop;

For its promised in one verse so sublime,

The contents of Galatians six: nine,

A harvest we'll reap, if we faint not.

The verse Roman's eight: eighteen,

Also embodies the assurance to be redeemed,

By a Creator whose word for Him to keep is a must;

Guaranteeing that if we do persist,

Submitting to God first, and the devil we resist,

Future glory shall be revealed to us.

So regardless of the venue,

Or in spite of what some may attempt to do,

To hinder with hardship or to bring trial.

With the coming of resistance,

To Godly plans, be persistent,

In doing so you'll overcome gile.

For one may surely forget it,

That hope to achieve victory without effort,

Is only aspiring unrealistically;

For those who truly achieve,

Realize that to bend their knees,

Is something needing to be done persistently.

And when all our efforts have been made,

and our progress has been assuaged,

And our discernment and judgement become unsober;

We have a mighty "triad,"

In whose hands we can be glad,

In which to seal victory, and to turn it over!

Howard E. Sims, Jr.

Untitled

It appears my pessimism,

Is in fact, truly realism,

With one standard on which to adhere;

The strength of revival,

Finds it's source in the Bible,

Life's only prototype to revere.

It's so very strange, That we often maintain,

That at some point and time, all is lost;

But when He stretched out and died,

and for His father he cried,

Oxymoronically He paid a good cost.

In this deadly sacrifice,

Was the attainment of life,

making no longer mandatory works on the scale';

For those accepting this feat,

There's no longer defeat,

With the wages of sin assuring hell!

Being perfect, and with no sin,

And enduring to the end,

My Saviour, helped me when I

had no chance;

To recover from a mistake of sin;

That my ancestral parents did begin,

That appeared so horrible at first glance.

At times so very disgusted,

At efforts I had mustered,

In attempts to straighten out my own life;

I soon came back to reality,

Through times just barely

When I give my problem(s) to Jesus Christ!

So my pesssimism is justified,

as by my life's circumstances I've been chided,

turning over my problems, things

Develop as they should;

For my Father has promised me,

for those loving the triad-trinity,

All things shall work out for the good,....

Ode #22

Some sin(s) we think, we can't even pare,

The essence without which,

Seems impossible to bare,

Most times we commence,

We abandon and give up,

In futile efforts our obsession(s) to disrupt.

Most severe in occurrence.

Are habitual afflictions.

Euphemistically characterized,

In terms like addictions (s).

These lifestyles

Though much harder to break or bend,

Irregardless of name.

Find their essence in sin!

So inadvertently if we wish to,

Escape from sin's habit, addiction, or flaw,

Deliverance is contingent on adherence to God's law;

Prayerfully we should approach the Saviour,

As our point to begin,

If we are to have any hope,

In our conquest of sin!

It's quit desturbing,
That i can't seem to shake,
the negative feelings,
In our blessing's; quake.

Lord can you help me,
be not so concerned.
About every happenstance
in our relationship i discern?

Give me the peace of mind,
That through you I can find,
Not to sulk at every incident,
To keep my heart sublime.

To take a minute,
to think, and not reflect of my beloved and others
In all things suspect.

Realizing, that in my infirmities,
Lord you've given me the ability to see,
Scenarios benefitting others,
And untold aid to my love through me!

So, as she and I march through,
her sobrietal trek,
let me retain positive intuition.
Eliminating negative suspect!

Ode #24

Although addiction is far from me,
This ode is being penned at a pub, named Murphy's
For me in such taverns, much time is spent,
Seeking the thoughtful solace,
Of a once familiar bent.

But now the partying,
In bars such as these,
Exists only
In vicarious memories.

But if you find yourself guessing,
I assure you, you're wrong
It's no longer, a season of pleasure,
For which I long.

To emit from by being.
The life I now embrace,
To assist the Lord,
To deliver his saving Grace.
To rapture those receptive,
Who are on the edge,
Of an ambivalent decision,
To escape from the dead,
That group of chemically dependent,

That at first, don't see,
That Satan's lured them to their doom,.
Quite insidiously.

For it did, to yours truly,
Happen for sure,
Through carnality and circumstance, I was snared by Satan's lure.

Appearing quasi-innocuous,
And then worlds of fun,
My inability to withdraw,
Became realization number one!
Nearly giving up,
But, not resigning to my fate,
in prayerful desperation.
I sought the "Master's" face.

As I once did also
Many choose not to stop.
To continue their delusion,
Instead they do opt.

But hopefully, as many will,
By His saving grace,
Shall end their relationship,
With the likes of Murphy's place.

Ode #25

It has now been initiated.

Progressing smoothly thus far,

Our plans to satiate,

An addiction thus to bar;

From the lives of us co-dependents,

Whose love helps impale,

The chemical to which one was dependent.

Causing the misery it did entail.

But with the aid of God,

Unceasing confidence will be gained,

For the recovery it won't be hard,

For "deliverance" to be claimed.

For just as her "freed" spouse,

Deliverance she will find,

If with sin she continues to joust,

Initially,....one moment at a time.

And when there's security,

And a degree of confidence,

There'll be a transition for her,

That'll evolve into "Deliverance.

Ode #26

"Altering Addiction"

The life of an addict must alter,

with the wood, stone and mortar,

Of his (of her) thinking and entire essence changed;

Only the minimal that remains pure,

Should he (or she) hold on for sure,

But all else should be altered, or not remain.

For whether we know it or not,

There's none that could stop,

Without god's spiritual hand or plan,

So for what the addict attempts to do,

And all other under takings too

For true success, "We must be born again.

Walking away, the young man couldn't give up,

Not allowing even Jesus to touch,

His wealth embraced as though a China doll'

Of the time, effort and cost,

Into the drugs of our choice,

We worship more than pagans of old, our modern gods.

For you see, it may seem cruel, or hard

That devotion to any, equal or more than God,

Becomes criteria for here of Scripture's greatest blasphemies;

But the amount of all we invest,

most surely does attest,

We love the chemicals and lifestyle more than Him-apparently.

Ode #27

I've seen 'em come,

I've seen 'em go,

I've seen 'em succeed and lose;

But my concern for her,

Shall be revealed, as it were,

For her sobriety is an exception i do choose.

Sometimes they stick,

The outcomes I predict,

Of one's success of failure in AA,

But with my fiancé' I do find,

That I cannot remain sublime,

And to expedite her success,

I must fervently pray.

There are no guarantees,

knowing after the struggling shall reap,

Aware that I can overcome all down periods through you!

Not meaning to veer, from God's guidance or direction,

My intentions, to some are not clear,

But their understanding may come, with little inspection.

For quite some time it's been the desire of my heart,

To walk with my fiancé in an upward trek toward God.

And sojourning our path,

With a mindset to accomplish that,

don't feel from her, I should run,

With every struggle or setback.

For every goal that's envisioned,

Such as a wedding day,

There must be made provision,

To warrant each to stay.

For without this conviction,

To the uncommitted it may seem odd,

to bring a goal to fruition,

Without the help of god!

And regardless of how it's embraced, attacked or condemned,

the honor is given to God this,

Christ-inspired poetry by Sims.....

Ode #28

This is a rendition,

That could cause division,

Between me and my "blue bird" fair;

Because a lack of honesty,

To her false promises,

To my sanity I must now give more care.

Attention to time,

She's never been inclined,

To consider a significant degree;

But not unlike others,

She almost shudders,

When made tardy by others like me.

I tarried my best,

In a countenance soon stressed,

In the past waiting for the before,

But her privilege I vow,

As I wait for her now,

For my nerves' sakes,

To wait no more!

Ode #29

Oh! Praise your name!

Oh! Father God,

Through you wisdom and your majesty;

There's been some strange effect on my life, unveiling...

Allowing me to see.

Progressive maturity,

Medical therapy,

Or, your sobrietal miracles,

Whether or not they be designated,

To you, all of them can be related,

As new salvational vehicles.

But honesty, at time,

In the purging process, I do find

Unpleasantries, and a perpetual annoyance;

And my spirit cries out to you,

As the discomforts ensue,

For utter and complete avoidance.

But Saviour!

My dear Saviour even with you there,

At times my eyes grow teary,

helping me endure,

I can be sure,

I won't faint, even though I be weary!

Devastating periods of depression,

Are countered by sporadic blessings,

Being introduced into my circumstances

And by others' presence it seems;

Allowing to enter, presumably blindly,

Your relief is always timely,

having one or more of these elements intervene.

So Lord! I'll hold on to the promises,

Of alcoholic's anonymous,

And especially, of course, The Bible too,

I'll cling and in my mind and keep,

Knowing after the struggling I shall reap,

Aware that I can overcome all down periods through you!

Ode #30

I'm going to be selfish,

I'm going to try and have my way,

I'm going to look within,

To her who has given pleasure everyday.

To try to hold onto her,

When the road I must trudge,

Because at least myself,

The Lord's made me hopelessly in love.

A few decisions, made correct,

But many I've made wrong

And because in her I suspect

I have strong desire to prolong,

The relationship between her and me,

Just as with her own plight,

To stay in a close proximity,

with her all my life.

Not meaning to veer,

From God's guidance or direction,

My intentions, to some are not clear,

But there understanding may come,

with little inspection.

For quite some time it's been,

The desire of my heart,

To walk with my fiancé,

In an upward trek toward God.

And sojourning our path,

With a mind set to accomplish that,

I don't feel from her, I should run,

with every struggle or setback.

For every goal that's envisioned,

Such as a Wedding Day,

There must be made provision,

for warrant each to stay,

For without this conviction,

To the uncommitted it may seem odd,

to bring a goal to fruition is impossible

With out the help of God!

Ode #31
ONE LAST THOUGHT

One last thought,

from the heart,

Just to impart,

Reverence to God!

Started by one whose life's problematic

Analyzed now, in a posture poetic.

With intentions of going beyond self therapy,

I implant godly revelations to my

Literary constituency,

With one viable and purposeful intent,

To show godly - Resolution,

To my efforts not ill-spent,

The essence of these memoirs,

From beginning to present posture,

Is one of mostly pain,

And occasional laughter

And regardless of how its embraced

Attacked, or condemned,

The honor is given to, it's essence in this

Christ - Inspired poetry by Sims,....

www.ingramcontent.com/pod-product-compliance
Lightning Source LLC
Chambersburg PA
CBHW030340290526
45785CB00004B/1549